Cats

by Helen Frost

Consulting Editor: Gail Saunders-Smith, Ph.D.

Consultant: Jennifer Zablotny, D.V.M.,
Member, American Animal Hospital Association

Pebble Books

an imprint of Capstone Press
Mankato, Minnesota

Pebble Books are published by Capstone Press
151 Good Counsel Drive, P.O. Box 669, Mankato, Minnesota 56002
http://www.capstone-press.com.

1 2 3 4 5 6 06 05 04 03 02 01

Library of Congress Cataloging-in-Publication Data
Frost, Helen, 1949–
    Cats/by Helen Frost.
    p. cm.—(All about pets)
    Includes bibliographical references and index.
    Summary: Simple text and photographs present cats and their basic care.
    ISBN 0-7368-0655-5
    1. Cats—Juvenile literature. [1. Cats. 2. Pets.] I. Title. II. All about pets (Mankato,
Minn.)
SF445.7.F76 2001
636.8—dc21

                                                                00-022989

Note to Parents and Teachers

The All About Pets series supports national science standards for
units on the diversity and unity of life. This book describes domesti-
cated cats and illustrates what they need from their owners. The
photographs support emergent readers in understanding the text.
The repetition of words and phrases helps emergent readers learn
new words. This book also introduces emergent readers to subject-
specific vocabulary words, which are defined in the Words to Know
section. Emergent readers may need assistance to read some words
and to use the Table of Contents, Words to Know, Read More,
Internet Sites, and Index/Word List sections of the book.

Table of Contents

4

Cats are pets.

Cats have four paws.

Cats have short hair
or long hair.

Most cats have
pointed ears.

Most cats have long tails.

Cats need food
and water.

Cats need a litter box.

Cats need a bed.

Cats need room to play.

food—something that people, animals, and plants need to stay alive and grow; owners should feed cats dry or canned cat food.

litter box—a container indoors for a cat to go to the bathroom; owners must clean litter boxes every day.

paw—the foot of an animal; most animals with paws have four feet and claws; cats need a place, such as a scratching post, to scratch with their claws; scratching keeps their claws short and sharp.

pet—a tame animal kept for company or pleasure

tail—the part at the back end of an animal's body; most cats have long, thin tails.

Bonners, Susan. *Why Does the Cat Do That?* New York: Henry Holt, 1998.

Hansen, Ann Larkin. *Cats.* Popular Pet Care. Minneapolis: Abdo & Daughters, 1997.

Schaefer, Lola. *Family Pets.* Families. Mankato, Minn.: Pebble Books, 1999.

Vrbova, Zuza. *Kittens.* Junior Pet Care. Philadelphia: Chelsea House, 1997.

Internet Sites

Cat Cabana
http://petstation.com/kittencare.html

Feline Public Library
http://acmepet.petsmart.com/feline/library

Kids' Korner
http://www.avma.org/care4pets/avmakids.htm

Pet Care
http://www.aspca.org/learn/petcare.html

Index/Word List

are, 5
bed, 19
ears, 11
food, 15
four, 7
hair, 9
have, 7, 9, 11, 13
litter box, 17
long, 9, 13
most, 11, 13

need, 15, 17, 19, 21
paws, 7
pets, 5
play, 21
pointed, 11
room, 21
short, 9
tails, 13
water, 15

Word Count: 43
Early-Intervention Level: 3

Editorial Credits
Martha E. H. Rustad, editor; Linda Clavel, designer; Jodi Theisen and Katy Kudela, photo researchers; Crystal Graf, photo editor

Photo Credits
International Stock/Tetsu Yamazaki, 6
Joan Balzarini, 8 (top), 10, 18
Norvia Behling, 1, 14, 16
Photo Network/Christine Pemberton, cover
Root Resources/Laurie Myhre-Choate, 4
Unicorn Stock Photos/Pam Power, 8 (bottom); Chris Boylan, 20
Visuals Unlimited/Bruce Gaylord, 12

The author thanks the children's section staff at the Allen County Public Library in Fort Wayne, Indiana, for research assistance. The author also thanks Nancy T. Whitesell, D.V.M., at St. Joseph Animal Hospital in Fort Wayne, Indiana.